I .. the solitude of the abyss, oh you, River Guadalevín! Wâdi-al-laban, you are the mute and silent witness of our history. Unconquerable and peaceful, your waters have formed the blanket of rocks and shapes which caress the gorge of our city, surrounding us with security and beauty depending on the historical airs due to your experiences; sometimes famed, sometimes reviled. Your need and direct participation in the annals of our city, have made you the reliable inheritor of our varied history. We have to turn to you in order to understand and comprehend the main historical, social and economic reasons for Ronda becoming a city.

The author

Publicaciones

RONDA 2000 S.L.

© Author: José Páez Carrascosa
© Publication and Production: Publicaciones Ronda 2000 S.L.
Translation: Katie Boyle
Photographic Composition: Edilux S.L.
© Layout, design and drawing: Miguel Román
© Photograph: J. Agustín Núñez
© Historical photos: Salvador Ordóñez "Cuso"
Printing: Copartgraf S.C.A.

Delivery by: Publicaciones Ronda 2000 S.L.
Phone number / Fax: 952 87 34 68
© The bandit drawing is the property of Publicaciones Ronda 2000 S.L.
ISBN: 84-932956-1-2
D.L.: GR-160/03

▪ Contents

Blas Infante Tiled Plaque
and outline of Historical
Andalusianism
Orson Welles Plaque
La Merced Convent
Square and Church of
Socorro
Chapel of Our Lady of
Sorrows
Giner de los Ríos
Monument

Los Descalzos Square and
Church

Las Peñas District
Rondan Balcony

San Sebastian Minaret

Holy Ghost Church
Almocábar and Charles V
Gates
Rupestrian church of Virgen de la Cabeza

CORDOBA

JAEN

SEVILLA

HUELVA

GRANADA

RONDA MALAGA

ALMERIA

CADIZ

Ronda from the district of Las Peñas

RONDA
in focus

Introduction
The History of Ronda
Ronda and its historical monuments

Ciudad de Ronda

•ENGRAVING OF RONDA.
Illustrations from 1649

•RONDA AND ITS DISTRICTS
It was the 16th and 17th Centuries that gave Ronda its current layout. The main part, Madinat began to be called 'The City'; the Alto District from then on the Espíritu Santo (Holy Spirit) District, and the Bajo District, abandoned by many of its inhabitants became the San Miguel District. The new areas of Mercadillo and San Francisco are symbols of new development and a new society.

•CUEVA DEL GATO *(right). Between the villages of Montejaque and Benaoján, which are famous for their pork sausages, we find La Cueva del Gato. (The Cave of the Cat)*

THE HISTORY OF RONDA

■ **RONDA IN ANTIQUITY**   Our town's land is a book where each strata shows us clearly the elements left behind by human beings, throughout 3,000 years of habitat.: Large pots, small pots, bowls, dolmen galleries and the vitally important casts for the Sa Idda swords. (7th century BC) We find tegulae, graves, silos,

gravestones, water courses, statues, amphorae, Roman inscriptions... hidden, covered over by the innumerable remains of Andalusian culture. According to Pliny they were surprised by the arrival of an unknown warlike people, the Bastulo Celts, who drank their waters in the 6th century BC and mixed with the other neighbouring people, the Iberians, eventually dominating the farthest corners of these mountainous lands. Greeks,

Carthaginians, Romans, Visigoths, Arabs and Berbers. All these races were forming this crucible of traditions, cultu-

res and history which make

up our Rondan society of today. The events are these: It was treason by the Praetor Galba and the subsequent rebelling followed by the death of Viriato that caused general Escipion Emiliano to found an equestrian legion (the "Legio Arundesis") in Arunda (Roman Ronda) in 139 BC He then ordered the construction of Laurus Cas-tle for obvious reasons: the pacification and control of Celtiberian tribes in the surrounding mountain ranges who were always on the point of rebelling and also to defend their privileges.

Under the protection of the

castle and its hanging white houses was created the first settlement and the start of our town of Ronda.

During the 1st century BC the outstanding figures from the Roman Empire, Sulla, Sertorio, Pompei and later Caesar and Octavio, claimed power supported by politi-cal parties. Sertorio, in his war against Pompeii destro-yed our town of Arunda and its Laurus Castle in 45 BC An altar was built, on the current site of Santa Maria de la Encarnación Church, to commemorate the victory of Gaius Julius Caesar over Cneo and Sexto, sons of Pompeii. Our history has always been diverse! Natural fortification with more than 500 metres of natural gorge, 170 metres deep and in a privileged situation at the crossroads of Roman roads coming from Cadiz, (via Zahara) and from Gibraltar (via the Guadiaro Valley.)

• ALMOCÁBAR "AL-MAQÂBIR" GATE, *cemetery gate 13th century. This was the main city gate and gave access to the Alto District, today known as the Espíritu Santo*

• SAN SEBASTIAN MINARET, *14th century. The only preserved minaret in Muslim Ronda.*

■ MUSLIM RONDA

The proximity to the Straits of Gibraltar, practically a day from the town, involved us from the start in Islamic invasions from North Africa. General Musa Ben Nusayr arrived in Spain in 712 and then his son, Abd al-Aziz, conquered our town and "El Laurel Castle" in 713, ordering the construction of the city of Izna-Rand-Onda on its ruins. Clearly the importance of our town, recognized by the new conquerors for its administrative organisation, made it the capital of Taco-ronna, one of the five coras or regions into which the South of Andalusia was divided. Berber tribes from the Atlas

mountains mixed with the indigenous population of Roman, Gothic and Hebrew origin. According to the historian Ibn Hazm, "To the area of Ronda and the Genal Valley there came the Wal-hasa, tribes from the mountains of North Africa with a minority of Arab families". Following the unfortunate reign of Hixen II, a Berber

lieutenant, Abú-Nur, taking advantage of the breakdown

of the Cordoban Caliphate, created the Taifa of the Ban Ifrán of Ronda constructing important buildings and reinforcing the city walls and defences. It is from this moment that Madinat Runda took on the urban shape that distinguishes it today.

The independence of Ronda did not last long. It was coveted by the kings of Malaga and those of Seville. Our Madinat will accompany them in its long historical journey until the unification of Al Andalus by the Almorávides and Almohades.

The Nazarite king, Muhamed II, cornered and fearful of the great Christian victo-

ries in Lower Guadalquivir and the great power of Castille, approaches the enemy, Abú Yusuf Yaqub in Fez, founder of the Marinite Empire to ask for his help in the face of sudden conquests, offering him in return, as compensation, the cities of Tarifa, Algeciras and Ronda in 1275

In 1295 the Marinites return to Morocco and give back to the Nazarite, Mohammad III, its Andalusian territories including Madinat Ronda. It was retaken by the Marinites in 1314, who then converted it into the key control point for the Straits of Gibraltar and the surviving Nazarite Kingdom because of its impregnable strength between the borders of the Christian Kingdoms of the Guadalquivir Valley, the Kingdom of Granada and North Africa. This unique and privileged position remained until its reconquest. However in 1340 the Marinites withdrew to their African territories and from then on our city pledged loyalty to the Kingdom of Granada until 1485.

• **Rainer Mª Rilke:**
""Ronda... is an incomparable region, a giant of rock on whose shoulders rests a city whitened and rewhitened with lime"

• **The Old Bridge.**
Drawn by Richard Ford 19th century. Romantic writers and artists expressed themselves and left their mark over its stones and paths.

• DAVID ROBERTS, *18th century illustration.*

• CONQUEST OF RONDA
Tableau in Toledo cathedral showing the assault on and conquest of Ronda by the Catholic Monarchs in 1485.

■ RONDA IN MODERN HISTORY

Following the conquest of Ronda 22nd May 1485 the lands were divided between the noblemen and knights who had taken part in the seizure of the city. On 25th July 1485 in Cordoba, Ronda was granted the right to rule itself by the same laws and privileges that Seville and Toledo had and to have the same royal house symbols: i.e. Consisting of a golden yoke with tethers and silver arrows on a red background.

The different Moorish uprisings in the mountain ranges and the lack of compliance with the terms of surrender following the conquest of Granada between King Boabdil and King Fernando and the expulsion decree of 31st March 1492 for unconverted Jews meant that our city never again occupied the same political, social and economic position; and many farms, villages and rural areas in the region were completely abandoned. The 16th and 17th

REINO DE FRANCIA
REINO DE NAVARRA
REINO DE ARAGON
REINO DE CASTILLA
REINO DE PORTUGAL
REINO DE GRANADA

• **VICENTE ESPINEL**
(1550-1624) Writer, poet, musician. He was a friend of Lope de Vega. (1562-1635), whom he called Master, and of Miguel de Cervantes (1547-1616). He added the fifth string, called the first string, to the Spanish guitar. As a poet he was the creator of the octosyllabic, a poetical form which he called "Espinela". As a writer he was the author of one of the masterpieces in Spanish literature during the Golden Century , the picaresque novel "El escudero Marcos de Obregón"

centuries saw the development of Ronda as we know it today. The main part, Madinat, began to be known as 'The City' The Alto District will be henceforth known as the Espíritu Santo District, and the Bajo or Jewish District where there were industries, tanneries and brothels will be known as the San Miguel District and dedicated to the Holy Cross.

The 18th century pointed our city towards the future. It enriched farming and industry as well as mining. Flourishing business, mainly around Gibraltar and the great increase in population gave rise to the construction of symbolic buildings in our city: Puente Nuevo, Felipe V Gate, Socorro Church, Santa Cecilia Church.... the laying down of the most important streets and squares of the new city.

The difficult situation created by the War of Independence (1808- 1812) followed by the absolutist period of Fernando VII, brought about an impoverished time for Ronda and its surroundings and the creation of bands of bandits and smugglers like the most famous characters in Andalusian banditry, José Maria el Tempranillo (1805-1833) However, the citizens of Ronda whose liberal tendencies are their most outstanding political characteristics, actively participated in the progress of contemporary history through its republican, liberal and conservative groupings; offering impeccable statesmen like Ríos Rosas, or avant garde teachers like Giner de los Ríos, founder of the 'Institución Libre' or being first in the province of Malaga to have a town council with a republican majority in 1891.

Distinguished visitors were received in Ronda during

• **ANA AMAYA MOLINA,** *Aniya the Gypsy, was born in Ronda 27 September 1885. She was a great singer and dancer. She was great aunt of the extraordinary artist Carmen Amaya. She sang and played the guitar all over Spain, in the best places and with the best singers of her time. Loved and respected by all, she knew artists and poets including Manuel de Falla and Federico García Lorca.*

• **DON FERNANDO DE LOS RÍOS,** *Illustrious Rondeño. (1879-1949), Minister of Public Education, Justice and State during the Second Republic. (Calle de los Remedios.)*

the complicated 19th century. The Duke and Duchess of Montpensier visited in 1849 and Empress Eugenia de Montijo, widow of Napoleon III in 1877. The century ended with long droughts and great social problems, accompanied by strikes, disorder and the ope-

ning of the railway in 1891. The 20th century was a century that promised future and development, tarnished by the civil war and the poor years that followed. Alfonso XIII visited on 4th March 1909. The city was given a new water supply system and a cemetery. Hotels were built. The Ronda Savings Bank was founded in February 1909 becoming the main savings organisation in Andalusia. The first Hispano American Congress on the single tax was held in Ronda in May

1913 and later in 1919 the city was where Andalusia established its bases with the creation of the Andalusian coat of arms and the green and white flag. Many pork processing factories, textile and furnishing factories and wine industry were established. Many cafes and cultural centres opened, reflecting the activity of a capital city where business with the villages in the area and around Gibraltar always was the main part of its activity. The end of the 20th century following the crisis during the 50's and 60's when half of the productive workforce was lost due to emigration and most of the craft workshops were abandoned, has seen decades during which a social and labour revitalisation has begun with the tourist influx into the city seeking the heritage and one of the best preserved natural environments in Andalusia.

Marquis of Salvatierra,
Side façade

RONDA
in focus

CITY WALLS AND XIJARA GATE, *11th century, in the centre the Church of Santa Maria la Mayor. 16-17th century*

(4) THE CITY HALL.
This was built in 1734 as barracks for King Felipe V's militia. From 1978 it has been the Casa Consistorial or Municipal building.

(9) ARAB BATHS
This is situated next to Las Culebras stream and San Miguel bridge. It consists of three halls, 13th –14th century.

RONDA AND ITS HISTORICAL MONUMENTS

Its privileged situation under the protection of the Tajo "with more than 500 metres of natural gorge, 170 metres deep" have given the city 3,000 years of history and some of the best preserved and important historical monuments in Spain.

(6) PLAZA DE TOROS DE RONDA
Sanctuary of Bullfighting on foot. It is the oldest Bullring in Spain for modern tauromachy. End of the 18th century.

(8) MONDRAGÓN PALACE
This was the residence of the Marinite King Abomelik, son of the Emperor of Fez, who was king of Ronda and Algeciras at the beginning of the 14th century.

(1) CHURCH OF SANTA MARIA LA MAYOR.
Erected on the old mosque.

Jardin
Blas Infan

(5) **HOUSE OF SAN JUAN BOSCO.** *(Overhanging house). Modernist style, very representative of Ronda's architecture and society at the beginning of the 20th century.*

(2) **MONUMENT TO THE MASTER ANTONIO ORDÓÑEZ** *by the sculptor Nicomedes Díez Piquero, 1996.*

(1) **CHURCH OF SANTA MARÍA.** *The Epistle Gate. Elegant Baroque from the 18th century. The entrance arch is framed by great thick pillars and niches with lion mastiffs in the recesses.*

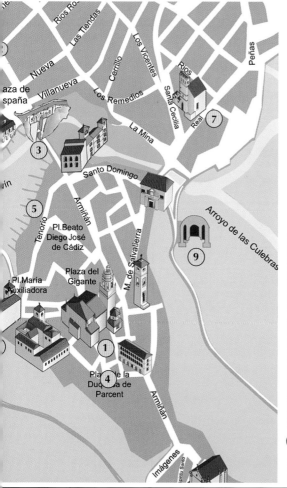

(3) **NEW BRIDGE** *18th century*

(7) **CHURCH OF PADRE JESÚS,** *in the old district of the Mercadillo. Its tower and façade are from the end of the 15 th century.*

RONDA

in focus

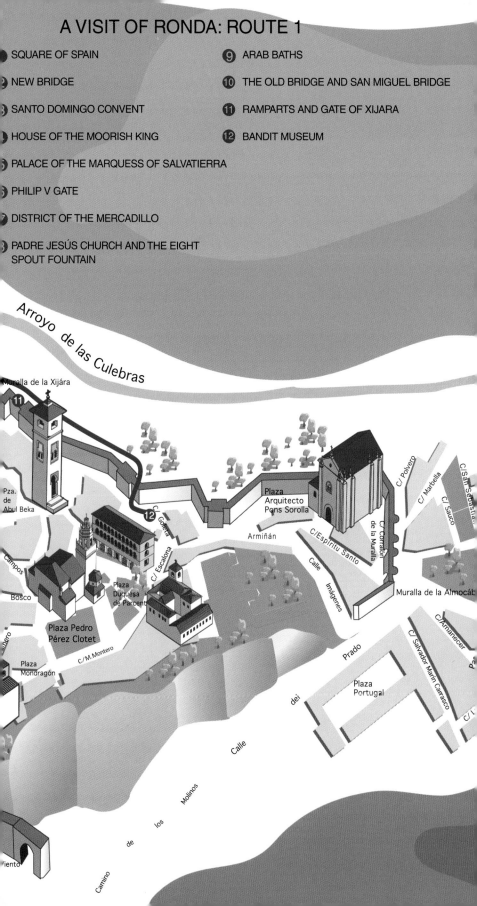

• **NEW BRIDGE** *and houses hanging over the Tajo.*

A visit of Ronda: Route 1

At certain times of the day, early mornings or at dusk, walking through the city is to encounter a magical and marvellous world that unite the human and the divine.

•**PLAZA DE ESPAÑA (SQUARE OF SPAIN). MONUMENT TO RÍOS ROSAS.**
To the right a bust of Don Antonio Ríos Rosas, Illustrious Rondan who became Minister and President of Congress in 1862.

■ **THE SQUARE OF SPAIN**
Built at the beginning of the 19th century, between the symbolical monuments of the Puente Nuevo and the Plaza de Toros. Its most representative building is the Parador de Turismo, 1994. Old Town Hall or Casa Consistorial from 1843. In the centre of the square is the monument to the memory of the Rondan, Don Antonio de los Ríos Rosas (1808 – 1873) Illustrious Statesman and honoured politician. He became a Member of the Spanish Parliament, Minister and President of the Congress in 1862.

He was the first member of a very important Rondan family which includes his nephew Don Francisco Giner

de los Ríos (1839 – 1915) liberal intellectual and creator of 'The Institución Libre de Enseñanza', and also his great nephew, Don Fernando de los Ríos (1879 – 1949) Minister of Public Education, Justice and State during the Second Republic and Ambassador to the United States during the Civil War.

■ THE NEW BRIDGE

This is the most representative monument of the city. Two great projects form this work. The first in 1735, during the reign of Felipe V, consisting of a great arch 35 metres in diameter, built in only 8 months but collapsed 6 years later, in 1741, – a catastrophe, killing 50 people.

A few years later (in 1751)

work began again, and was finished in 1793 coinciding

with the Royal Festival in May. This means that it took 42 years to build. Leading the construction was Don José Martin Aldehuela, an architect from Manzanera, in the province of Teruel, Aragon.

• **PUENTE NUEVO.**
Photo 1918.
This masterly work is 98 metres high, built with stone ashlars highlighting its foundations from the bottom of the gorge. It is formed from three sections; its lower part is an archway on which rest the central arch that reaches 90 metres.

• **INSIDE THE BRIDGE,** *in the central part there is a room of approx 60 mts. which has had several uses throughout its long 200 year history, the most famous of which was its use as a prison for dangerous prisoners.*

• **OVERHANGING HOUSES;** *in the background the area of La Albacara. Inside the walled grounds was the area for enclosing the cattle from the surrounding area when the alarm sounded or the city was besieged.*

This masterly work is 98 metres high, built with stone ashlars highlighting its foundations from the bottom of the gorge. It is formed from 3 bodies, its lower part is an archway on which rests the central 90 metre arch with two smaller side arches supporting the street level. In the central part there is a room of approx. 60m which has had several different uses throughout its long 200 year history, the most famous of which was its use as a prison for dangerous prisoners. Its original entrance was the

square building on its left and was used as a watch

tower. With regard to the legend that the architect committed suicide or fell over the edge of the gorge once the bridge was completed, it is necessary to clarify that Don José Martín Aldehuela, on finishing the bridge went to Malaga where he became the master architect and died in that city in 1802. He was buried in the Church of Santiago at the age of 80. In the middle of this significant monument is the Puente Nuevo Interpretation Centre.

• **AERIAL VIEW OF THE PUENTE NUEVO.**

• **PARADOR NACIONAL** *(1994) Above*
Built on the same edge of the precipice. It is built on plots of land which used to be the Town Hall (1837- 1978); Alhóndiga or public market (1930) – 1980) and the very popular summertime cinema "Tajo Cinema" between the 50's and 70's.

• **CONVENT GATE** *In front of one of the many springs of the "céntimo fountain" that form part of the Rondan townscape until the beginning of the 20th century. Photo from Cuso files.*
Santo Domingo Convent. (Photo below).

■ Santo Domingo Convent.

Founded by order of the Catholic Monarchs. Once the building was completed, the chapel and the convent came under the patronage of Dominican Friars, with dedication to St. Peter Martyr.

The building is a mixture of Gothic, Mudéjar and Renaissance, although all that remains of the original building is the church and part of the cloisters. The church's entrance is on Calle Santo Domingo; it is simple and in stone. Its doorway has two shields, one of the Dominican Order and the other of the Holy Office, because the convent housed the court of the Holy Inquisition. It consists of three naves with an elevated half orange, highlighting its beautifully coffered, polychromed Mudéjar ceiling.

During the 16th and 17th Centuries it was one of the most influential churches in the city. In 1850 it became the first covered market and corn exchange in Ronda.

■ **THE HOUSE OF THE MOO-RISH KING.** This 18th century building has changed structure (and owners) over the years until the current form was crea-

ted by the Duchess of Parcent in 1920.

Its gardens were designed by the French architect Jean Claude Forestier, creator of the Maria Luisa Park in Seville or the Bois de Boulogne in Paris. Most worthy of mention is the famous underground passage "La mina". Built at the start of the 14th century. Part of it was built in the natural rock and part in masonry and bricks in arches and vaults with some holes and windows to let in the light. Its access is through a door in the gardens of the house, from where a 365 step staircase leads off, although now it has only 200 steps. Inside, one can appreciate, apart from a beautiful piece of engineering, several rooms or openings like dungeons, a gallery with

•FAÇADE OF THE HOUSE OF THE MOORISH KING.

• TILED PLAQUE. *Represents an Arab king, perhaps Abomelik, in a hieratic pose, hence the incorrect name of "The House of the Moorish King".*

• **THE DUCHESS OF PARCENT.** *Doña Trinidad Schultz, a woman of great beauty and intelligence, bought the house from Mr. Perrin of Baltimore, U.S.A, at the beginning of the 20th century. She enriched it with the best quality furniture, paintings and ceramics which she brought from all over the world. It was visited by the most important families of that period, giving Ronda great social significance.*

• **CALLE SANTO DOMINGO** *(above), the street where the house is located.*

half pointed arches to store water and grain and the hall of the secrets with a very interesting semi circular vault leading directly onto the well which is filled with water coming from the Guadalevín.

• THE BROKEN PEDIMENT held up by four nude Indians, a mannerism of a certain colonial style, where the boys are laughing and sticking out their tongues, whilst the girls try to hide their embarrassment at being naked.

■ **THE MARQUESS DE SALVATIERRA PALACE.** Its Baroque façade dating from 1798, in stone masonry. The door has a lintel with Corinthian columns and a large Rondan wrought ironwork balcony. It is enriched by a broken pediment held up by four Indians, a mannerism of a certain colonial style, where the boys are laughing and sticking out their tongues whilst the girls are trying to hide their embarrassment at being naked. In the middle is the coat of arms of the family headed by Vasco Martín de Salvatierra, contino of the Catholic Monarchs following the conquest of Ronda.

The houses are whitewashed to cleanse them and keep them fresh during the long Summer periods; the wrought iron in the windows and balconies are protective features which have made Ronda an example of sober and beautiful popular Andalusian architecture.

• **THE BALCONY.**
(on the left side of the Palace). Silent witness to the historical film - making in Spanish cinema, such as : Carmen, la de Ronda, Las Sabinas, Amanecer en Puerta Oscura, Curro Jimenez, the Opera Carmen...

Its interior represents the simplicity of Rondan houses of the 17th and 18th centuries. It has notable furnishings from different periods, some historical Sevillian tiles from the 17th century in the family dining room and a small garden with a magnificent Spanish fir, which complete and justify the artistic interest in this house. To the left a photograph of the secluded and enchanting corner of the city, dominated by the stone cross marking the encampment of the Marquess of Cadiz in the taking of Ronda. The cross was brought to this spot in 1965 during the restoration of the old town by the architect Don Francisco Pons Sorolla.

This house combines the most characteristic features of Rondan architecture : the wrought iron grill, whitewash and stone.

■ PHILIP V GATE

Following the collapse of the first Puente Nuevo in 1741, the need to improve this entrance became apparent. This was due to the great influx of people and goods plus the use of new means of transport which had to use the entrance. The old Arab Gate on the bridge was replaced by the more convenient current gate, which is larger, during the reign of the first Bourbon on the Spanish throne, Felipe V in 1742; according to the stone next to the gate. It consists of a double masonry arch, crowned by three pinnacles and adorned by the Anjou shell and royal shield of the Bourbons on the outside.

Through its archway one of the most revealing and romantic images of the new city or old street market can be enjoyed. Centre of commercial activity during the 16th, 17th and 18th centuries, it is the romantic district for writers, poets, painters and travellers who have visited it throughout its long modern history.

Its current appearance is due to restoration work in 1960.

• **FELIPE V GATE** *and in the background the Xijara gate seen from the Padre Jesus district.*

Above, photo of the gate in 1940, with a popular personality of that time, "El Panadero Callejero" (the Street Baker).

• THE MARKET DISTRICT

It is certain that a poor district existed in this Northern part of the Madinat next to the Puente Viejo or Arab Bridge, at the exit of one of its main gates, "la Puerta de la Puente" where the road to Granada starts. However the birth of this extra – mural district, with its own personality, began with the reconquest of the city by the Catholic Monarchs. To the right Felipe V Gate. (1742)

■ The Mercadillo District.

The mandate of the Catholic Monarchs " No Jew will live in Ronda, nor stay here for

more than three days, except Israel, our translator of Arabic". The sharing out of land and houses amongst those who had participated in the conquest of Ronda and expulsion edict of 31st March 1492 for the unconverted brought a great population

centre to the plains outside the walls of the city, today known as San Francisco and Mercadillo Districts. Condi-

tions deteriorated when Doña Margarita of Austria gave back her powers over Ronda to the Crown on moving to Flanders as Governess in 1499. During these times the administration and government of the city suffered great changes. New laws and sales tax enforced on tradesmen and merchants on entering the city, forced them to settle outside the city walls.

• **PADRE JESÚS CHURCH** was origi-nally dedicated to Santa Cecilia.

■ PADRE JESUS CHURCH.

The tower façade is from the original building from the end of the 15th to the beginning of the 16th century. Its stone Gothic gateway is finished off with a Renaissance bell tower with three half pointed arches. The church is not very spacious but it is well laid out. It is divided into three naves separated by brick columns and two columns back to back on each side supporting the six half point arches forming the central nave. This is higher with an exuberant plaster decoration hiding a beautiful Mudéjar coffered ceiling dating from the restorations

of 1769. In this parish, notable

Rondans were baptised, such as the writer Vicente Espinel, the politician Ríos Rosas, or the bullfighter, Cayetano Ordóñez "Niño de la Palma" Inside is the beautiful image of Padre Jesús Nazareno (left). It enjoys great popularity with a special devotion every Friday of the year.

•**EIGHT SPOUT FOUNTAIN.** *Located in Calle Real; it evokes the glorious past of this district, the first commercial and social centre of Christian Ronda upto the middle of the 19th century. It is made of stone with two fronts, one with eight spouts from which it gets its name; and the other with a large water trough for animals. It was built by King Felipe VI during the middle of the 18th century.*

a wall and has a tower at the back which had a waterwheel, that no longer exists, to raise water from the stream and then to send it via a small aqueduct over arches to the bathing halls.

At the entrance in front of the old horseshoe arched doorway there is the pool or washing fountain, which is today in open bricks laid horizontally and very well preserved, which was used for cleansing before entering the main building.

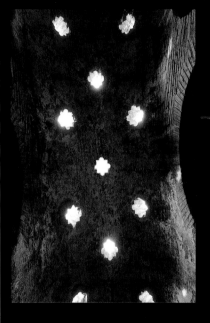

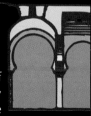

■ ARAB BATHS

These were built between Las Culebras Stream and the Rio Grande, the perfect place to easily channel water, in Bajo or Jewish District at the end of the 8th century. Despite the plundering they suffered, they are one of the best preserved throughout Spain. The building is enclosed by

■ STRUCTURE

The baths consist of three rooms easily recognized for their use and structure. In the first hot room was the boiler to heat the water, which came from the waterwheel, with a chimney for the outlet of smoke; in essence it was the service room. The system used was inherited from the Romans, consisting of: heating the water in situ, passing the

lights in the form of stars and facing East to West, so that the sunlight enters perfectly during the daylight hours. Its perfect preservation makes us stop to admire this room. In the third room there is a large font of cold water. The room can be entered from either side and was a room for relaxing, massages and dressing.

hot steam under the floor through channels to the central room
The second, central, room is divided into three naves covered by semi – circular coffered ceilings on brick horse shoe arches. It is lit by sky-

Photographs of the Arab Baths early 20th century.

• THE SPANISH FIR.
(located in the Plaza del Campillo or Maria Auxiliadora) Abies Pinsapo Boissier, a plant from the Tertiary era. It is the most Southern European fir and the oldest of all species of Mediterranean firs. This living fossil can be found throughout the areas of: Sierra de las Nieves, Yunquera or in the woods of Genalguacil and Casares, and in the Reales de Sierra Bermeja, all of which are in the province of Malaga. It is also found in the Sierra del Pinar between Grazalema and Benamahoma, in the province of Cádiz.
• ALAMEDA DEL TAJO, *to the right, on a postcard from the forties.*

■ THE OLD BRIDGE

Its origin is Arabic. According to some authors it was constructed during the time of Abomelic, the King of Ronda; and according to others during the time of Mohamed III of Granada. What is certain is that following the seizure of Ronda by the Christians it had to be urgently repaired again in 1616. It consists of one single arch, 10 metres diameter by 31 metres high, above the level of the river, 30 metres long and 5 wide. In 1961 it was restored again, the balconies were opened and adorned with iron-work balls which gave it its current appearance.

■ SAN MIGUEL BRIDGE

Next to the Holy Cross Chapel, old synagogue and Arab Baths.

Although of Arab origin it is commonly known as Roman.

■ **THE CITY WALLS, 11ᵀᴴ CENTURY.** On the death of Almansor, one of his lieutenants created the independent Taifa of Banu Ifran of Ronda. For 40 years he governed his kingdom in peace and improved and made buildings and walls like Xijara to defend themselves against the greed of the neighbouring Berbers.

■ **THE XIJARA GATE.**
Used to link the Bajo or Jewish District with the City and together with its walls is the best preserved. It occupied a middle point between the first exterior wall with four preserved towers and the inner or main wall. In 1975 it was rebuilt similar to that of the Almocábar gate with three arches, two horse - shoe shaped and one pointed with an open space between the first and second.

•**THE EASTERN PART OF THE CITY**
In this photograph we can see from all the preserved remains that it had to be a

very important area in the Islamic city.

- **IN THE MUSEUM** *the room dedicated to the Guardia Civil is outstanding. It was founded by the Rondan Duke Ahumada in 1844 with a varied collection of documents, photographs and historical information on the Guardia Civil from its foundation until today.*

BANDIT MUSEUM.

Here we can find, in chronological order, the world of banditry in all its historical facets from its origins: Diego Corriente (1757-1781) Juan Caballero (1804-1885), José Maria "el Temprani-llo"(1805-1833), the seven boys of Écija (1812- 1818),the kidnappers of Andalusia (1869-1871)... up to the last bandit of the Rondan district, Juan Mingolla "Pasos Largos" (1873-1934)

There are also numerous historical descriptions of romantic travellers, lots of documents and reproductions of caves, grottoes and kidnappings.

• *Rondan Windows*

RONDA
in focus

A VISIT OF RONDA: ROUTE 2
CITY HALL
MARIA AUXILIADORA CHURCH
SANTA ISABEL CHURCH AND CONVENT
COLLEGIATE CHURCH OF SANTA MARÍA
(CATHEDRAL)
MONDRAGÓN PALACE
JOAQUÍN PEINADO MUSEUM
OUR LADY OF PEACE CHURCH
HOUSE OF ST. JOHN BOSCO

ROUTE 2

1. CITY HALL
2. MARÍA AUXILIADORA CHURCH
3. SANTA ISABEL CHURCH AND CONVENT
4. COLLEGIATE CHURCH OF SANTA MARÍA (CATHEDRAL)
5. MONDRAGÓN PALACE
6. JOAQUÍN PEINADO MUSEUM
7. OUR LADY OF PEACE CHURCH
8. HOUSE OF SAINT JOHN BOSCO

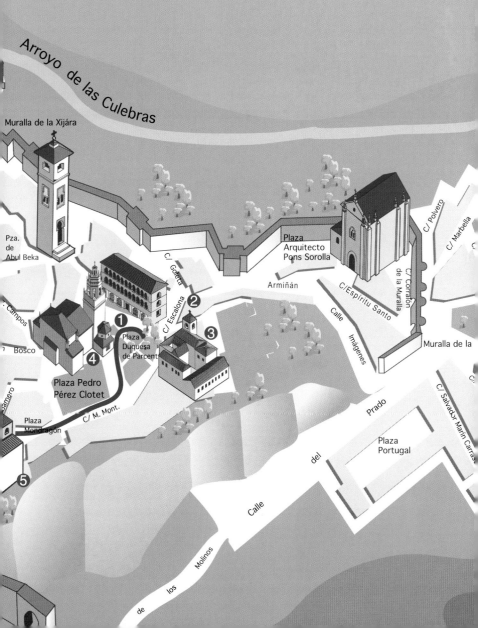

A VISIT OF RONDA: ROUTE 2

The quietness of your nights ¡Oh, Plaza de la Ciudad! Imbued with airs of the souks, duels and jousts, of writers and poets.

• ST. ISABEL OF THE ANGELS, *below, religious convent under the order of Saint Clair, built in 1540 on the site that the prison and water store occupied during the Islamic domination.*

■ **THE RONDA TOWN HALL**
Built in 1743 to house the 28th Regiment of the Provincial Regiments founded by King Felipe V. It is built on what used to be the old shops of this Plaza Mayor. At the rear are the Viejo Pósito (Communal Granary), The Alhóndiga (Corn Exchange), and the Panadera Mayor (Royal Bakers) from the 16th century; forming the most important urban area of the city and are integral parts of the actual Municipal Building. A few years ago these buildings were remode-

lled to convert them into the new Municipal Government building in 1978 preserving the original beauty and enriching it with a 16th century Mudéjar coffered ceiling. Its

entrance is made up of a flat door between pillars. On the left hand side the shield with the chalice and star of the city

of Cuenca, which is twinned with Ronda, and on the right hand side the shield of our city granted by the Catholic Monarchs. (left)

• **THE MARIA AUXILIADORA CHURCH,** built in 1950, encloses the square to the south (photo below). An extremely popular church dedicated to the Virgen Mary. The Sale-

sian College of Sagrado Corazón de Jesus (Sacred Heart of

Jesus) was founded by the Marquises of Moctezuma at the beginning of the 20th century. It has been the keystone of Rondan education from its foundation to date. It is situated on the old Laurel Castle which was ordered to be built in 132 BC by General Escipión Emiliano and destroyed by the French during the War of Independence in 1812.

• TOWN HALL.
Worthy of a visit in this building are: The

Council Chamber (Salón de Plenos) and, in the basement, the floor of the old Corn Exchange.

•THE CATHOLIC MONARCHS *granted Ronda the symbols of the Royal Family: a golden yoke with cut tethers and silver arrows on a red background. (previous page)*

45

•Plaza Mayor.
Called the Square of the Duchess of Parcent and also the City Square. In the centre is the monument to the Duchess of Parcent, (1866 –1937)

Collegiate Church of Santa María

On the site where the main Friday mosque was until the reconquest of 22nd May 1485, was built the Cathedral by King Fernando, the Catholic. It is situated on the highest part of the city where there used to be a Roman altar in memory of Julius Caesar to commemorate his victory over the sons of Pompeii, Cneo and Sexto, in the battle of Munda in 45 BC. At the end of the 9th century the Arabs built an Aljama or main mosque, whose current remains are the location of the Mudéjar tower, today a bell tower and the remains of the Mihrab Arch. This Mudéjar, exposed brick bell tower, early 16th century, is built on the base of the old

minaret of the Mosque and some of the original building material was included

in its construction.

Some beautiful balconies built during the reign of Felipe II (photo above) cover the main door of the primitive Gothic church. These balconies were used for the nobility and the city authorities to watch jousts, bull fights and other public events. The Gothic church was built at the end of the 15th /early 16th centuries. It is late Gothic with three naves separated by pointed arches and a single capitel decorated with thistles and phantasmic and anthropomorphic animals.

In the centre of the nave is the chapel altarpiece, to the right of the altar, a fresco of St. Christopher by the Rondan artist José de Ramos, in 1798 and to the left, the altarpiece to the Virgen de Mayor Dolor. (Our Lady of Sorrows)

In 1580 an earthquake severely

• **Casita de la Torre** *(Little House of the Tower). At the foot of the bell tower (below). A pretty Mudéjar building used as a small chapel separate from the main building. It has several small roofs at different heights and directions, and some beautiful horseshoe arches on the front.*

•THE EPISTLE DOOR.
Above. Exterior of the Church of Santa Maria. Elegant Baroque from the 18th century. The entrance arch is framed by thick pillars and niches embellished by winged lions in the alcoves.

• THE MIHRAB ARCH,
photo right, is located at the rear of the Chapel Altar, decorated with vegetal, geometrical and calligraphic atauriques from the Nazarite dynasty, from the end of the 13th/ early 14th century, reminiscent of the oratories in the Alhambra of Granada.

affected the structure of the central nave and the Mudéjar craftsmanship was replaced by four semicircular vaults on pendentives with motives of the litanies. Afterwards when the north wall of the church capsized, construction was started on a Renaissance nave similar to those of the Cathedrals in Granada and Malaga,

side naves are covered by ribbed vaults at right angles and the chapels by four spherical roofs. The Baldaquin in Canadian red pine is a highlight; a fine example of Rondan carving from the beginning of the 20th century. To the left, the main altar of Nuestra Señora de la Cabeza. The image is a beautiful 18th century car-

with Corinthian and Tuscan columns. It was built between 1584 and 1704. This part of the church is composed of a basilical nave with a central vault and five side vaults. The central nave is covered by a segment of a sphere with eight ribs and a large central medallion. The

ving. It is venerated from the beginning of September to the second Sunday in June when it is transferred in a procession to the hermitage of Cave of San Antón, an old Mozarabic church, built between the 10th and 11th centuries on the outskirts of the city.

The Annunciation

The Nativity

Mary Mother

The Resurrection

• **NTRA. SRA. REINA DE LA FAMILIA**
(Our Lady, Queen of the Family) situated in the retro-choir altar, by Antonio J. Dube

Maria de la Encarnación, requested the Vatican to include in the litanies, the invocation "Queen of the family, pray for us" ; a request that

• **THE VIA LUCIS MARIANO** *includes 14 stations in bronze by the sculptor Francisco Parra, born in 1961 in Seville. Above pictures.*

Choir, 1736

de Luque, Sevillian artisan of religious images, May 1977. In 1994, the year of Santo Mariano, Don Gonzalo Huesa Lope, parish priest of the Real Colegiata de Santa

was granted by Pope John Paul II towards the end of that year.

• **ALTAR OF VIRGEN DEL MAYOR DOLOR,** *left, old altar of relics. Gilt and Churrigueresque altar, it is presided over by Our Lady of Sorrows, by Maria Luisa Roldan, "La Roldana", sculptor to Carlos II, end of 17th century.*

• **O**IL **P**AINTING OF THE **C**RUCIFIXION.
Photo below.
A modernist touch in the Gothic Church. Murals are by the French painter Raymonde Pagégie: The Life of St. Peter, The Conversion of St. Paul, The Apocalypse, The Crucifixion and the Last Supper were painted by the Parisian artist between 1982 and 1988.

• **A**LTAR OF THE **T**ABERNACLE IN THE **G**OTHIC NAVE.
Beautiful Baroque from the beginning of the 18th century and finished in gold in 1773. Outstanding are the four Salomonic columns decorated with vines and fruit, that divide the altarpiece into 3 sections. The altarpiece is crowned by a high relief of the Incarnation and in the centre, the niche with the Immaculate Virgen. On

the previous page, detail of the choir in Manneristic Baroque style; 1736.

Renaissance nave of the church (photo above). Of basilical ground plan with harmonious proportions are its architectural features. The most striking of all is its Baldaquin in red Canadian pine, beginning of the 20th century.

MONDRAGÓN PALACE

Residence of the Marinite King Abomelik when king of Ronda and Algeciras in the 14th century and palace of the last Arab Governor of the city, Hamed el Zegrí. It was occupied by the king himself on his return to Ronda in 1501. Later the property passed to the Valenzuela family. One of its members, the first Marquess of Villasierra, "the Imp of the Palace" was the favourite of Mariana de Austria, widow of Felipe IV and favourite of King Charles II. This is the most important palace of the civil architecture of the city. Part of the layout of the gardens and the entrance of the passage that joined the Muslim house with the old fortress still remains. Its monumental façade is in sandstone and has two pairs of 14th century Doric columns supporting a second horseshoed body from the beginning of the 17th century. Its opening is flanked by Ionic pillars; a doorway with iconography of the insignia of the Virgen Mary. The front is flanked by two exposed brick Mudéjar towers and half pointed arches, finished off with a roof of four slopes.

Its first patio or Aljibe patio, from the 18th century, leads us to the Mudéjar patio, the most important one in the palace,

• **AMONG THE WHITE HOUSES** *there is a particularly stately one, commonly known as "The Stone House". It is a clear display of the cultures, styles and civilizations of Rondan civil architecture.*

- **PATIO FROM THE 16 TH CENTURY.** *It is the clearest exponent of Rondan Mudejar.*

- **THE GARDEN**
Through the horseshoe arch there is a garden where the water from the fountains break the Andalusian garden's silence. To the right the parapet of the well. 18th century patio.

housing the Municipal Archeological Museum: brick half pointed arches decorated with Renaissance tiles supporting a wooden gallery whose walls still conserve parts of the Renaissance frescos which decorated the building in the 16th century. Also worthy of mention is the Mudéjar coffered ceiling in the first floor noble salon, 16th century. Through a horseshoe arch there is a small garden with a lovely view of the San Francisco District. Inside the Municipal Archeological Museum there are interesting lithic and metallurgical stones and the mold to make the Sa-Idda bronze swords, 7th century B.C. and the very rich and extensive exhibits of Andalusian funeral artefacts.

Wandering along Calle San Juan Bosco, at n° 11, we see the small palace of Hinojo-

sa Bohórquez whose patio has the most beautiful tiles in the city. In front, the old palace of the Marquesses of las Amarillas and Dukes of Ahumada, Viceroys in Nueva España and founder of the Guardia Civil. We continue until we reach the Palace of the

Marquesses of Moctezuma, heirs to the Ovalles Estate. This building was occupied by King José Bonaparte in 1810 and is currently the Joaquín Peinado Museum (left) created by the Unicaja de Ronda Foundation with a permanent collection of oil paintings and drawings by this Rondan painter. (Ronda 1898 – Paris 1975) In front of the House of the Giant, a representative mansion of the Rondan middle class in the 14th century, the patio with a well, and decorated inside with vegetal ➡

• **WALKING THROUGH THE STREETS.**
Walking down this street is to relive the past atmosphere of the city of Lower Andalusia. Its heraldry and grills make us carry on until we reach the back of the Church of Santa Maria. On arrival we immediately see a wrought iron cage of the Perez Girón house, evoking the ironwork of Ronda and old gallantry, damsels and furtive encounters.

• **CHURCH OF OUR LADY OF PEACE**
This church is dedicated to the Patron saint of Ronda. The tradition comes from the time of King Alfonso XI, who, on abandoning the siege of the city, left a statue for the invocation of the Mozarabics of the area, although the present statue is from the end of the

• **THE CARVING**
Detail of an ancestral house with traditional Rondan carving giving its name to one of the few preserved pieces of craftsmanship in the city. "The Rondan Furniture".
Hotel San Gabriel.

■ **CHURCH OF THE VIRGEN DE LA PAZ. (OUR LADY OF PEACE)**
The present church dates from the end of the 17th /early 18th century, consisting of a single nave whose Mudéjar coffered ceiling was covered with a semi barrelled Baroque vault with a semi circular cupola over the presbytery and a small cupola with a lantern. Its façade is from the end of the 16th century with a stone doorway and semi pointed arch finished off with an 18th century belfry. This façade has 18th century sculptures of rosettes and stars remarkable for their colour and relief. In this church are the remains of Blessed Friar Diego José de Cadiz in a silver urn at the feet of the Virgen Mary.

motifs on the walls and spandrels. On the façade there is a Melkar sphinx, a Punic Hercules. Then there is the Holgados old family palace from the 18th century, restored and converted into the San Gabriel Hotel. To the left the church of the Virgen de la Paz, in front of which is the house where Blessed Friar Diego José de Cadiz died in 1801.

■ **THE HOUSE OF SAN JUAN BOSCO.**

Finally we finish our walk at one of the most beautiful and enchanting spots of our city. The house has a Nazarite tiled patio(right) and a very good example of regional ceramics. Noteworthy is the collection of bullfighting tiles by the great ceramist from Cuenca P.Mercedes.

It was built in a modernist style at the beginning of

the 20th century by the architect Santiago Sangui-

netti and belonged to the Granadinos family, who

• **THE GARDEN**

A visit to the garden is obligatory. An orchard at the edge of the precipice, overhanging the void by the whim of human will. It is enriched with tiles, mosaics, marble and fountains, directing us to face the most representative monument of Ronda; the Puente Nuevo.

• **Reiner Maria Rilke**
In this corner of paradise we evoke people like Rainer Mª Rilke, who in his Spanish Trilogy wrote " Ronda is an area without comparison, a rock giant supporting a small city on its shoulders..."

•**James Joyce**,
Who finished his masterpiece Ulysses in our city: " Ronda with its old windows..., its narrow streets..., and its gardens of roses and jasmine, geraniums and cactus";

gave it to the Salesian Order to be used as a rest home for old and ill priests from the order. The beautiful patio

plete collection of regional ceramics, the highlight of which is the collection of bullfighting panels by the

with its Nazarite tiles (photo previous page) and a com-

great Cuencan ceramist P.Mercedes in the solarium

gallery. Also, the tapestries from the Royal Factory, 19th century and its walnut furniture, chimney, bureau, dining room..., the purest Castillian style of our Rondan furniture.

The view from this house of the Guadalevín Valley with its mills and market gardens " land of pears and quinces", brings us to the Walls of the Albacara, 13th century. Located where the precipice is more than 100 mts. deep, forming this part of the natural defence system of the Tajo. This external barrier was essentially a second exterior wall and corral for the livestock in times of danger and sieges. It consisted of two gates, The Puerta del Viento that connected the valley with the Albacara and Puerta de los Molinos or Christ's Arch which gave access to the bottom of the Tajo with its mills and olive oil presses.

• **ERNEST HEMINGWAY**

... and we shall meet face to face the abrupt beauty of the Tajo, which Ernest Hemmingway described so uniquely in his book "Death in the Afternoon": It is to Ronda where you have to go, if you ever go to Spain. The whole city and its surroundings are a romantic decoration. A pretty spot. It has been built in a circle of mountains on a plateau; the plateau is cut by a gorge which divides it into two cities...., after the bullfights they carry the dead horses to the edge of this rocky place where the birds, who have been waiting for their turn all day, fling themselves on the remains."

•PLAZA DE TOROS,
corrida goyesca.

RONDA
in focus

A VISIT OF RONDA: ROUTE 3
BULL RING
BLAS INFANTE PROMENADE AND ALAMEDA PARK
TILED PLAQUE TO BLAS INFANTE
REVIEW OF ANDALUSIAN HISTORY
PLAQUE TO ORSON WELLES
CONVENT OF LA MERCED
SOCORRO SQUARE AND CHURCH
CHAPEL OF OUR LADY OF SORROWS
MONUMENT TO GINER DE LOS RÍOS
LOS DESCALZOS SQUARE AND CHURCH
LAS PEÑAS DISTRICT
RONDAN BALCONY

On the left, Bullring. Goyescan Bullfight. September.

ROUTE 3

1. BULL RING
2. BLAS INFANTE PROMENADE AND ALAMEDA GARDENS
3. ORSON WELLES PLAQUE
4. CONVENT OF LA MERCED OR CARMELITE SISTERS
5. SQUARE AND CHURCH OF OUR LADY OF SOCORRO
6. CHAPEL OF OUR LADY OF SORROWS
7. GINER DE LOS RÍOS MONUMENT
8. LOS DESCALZOS SQUARE AND CHURCH
9. LAS PEÑAS DISTRICT
10. RONDAN BALCONY

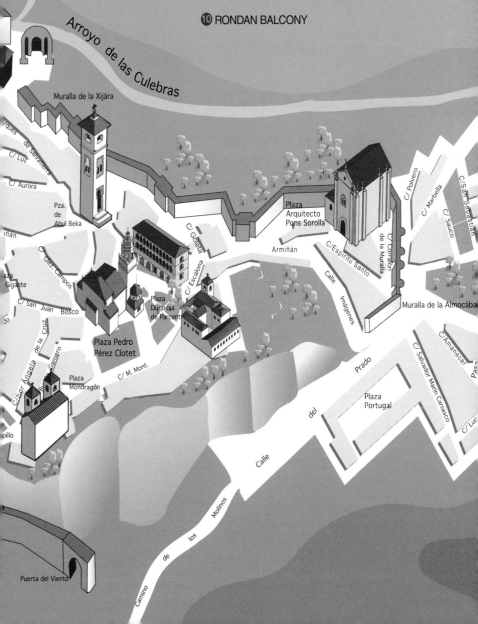

■ RONDA'S BULLRING

A sanctuary for bullfighting on foot, it is the oldest preserved bullfighting building. It opened in May 1784 , but the collapse of part of the stands meant that it had to be restored and it reopened for the festival of May 1785, with the participation of Pedro Romero and his rival Pepe Hillo. It belongs to the Real Cuerpo de la Maestranza de Caballería de Ronda, (Royal Corps of the Institute of Knights of Ronda) Felipe II, 1572.

The ring forms a perfect circle with double arcades of depressed arches on 136 Tuscan columns, different to the Royal balcony which has more profuse decoration and fluted columns. It has 5,000 seats, a stone barrier and a 66m. diameter ring.

There are few bullfights nowadays. During the second week of September there is the traditional Goyescan bullfight in memory of Pedro Romero (1754 - 1844) It has all the rules of the modern bullfight. Pedro Romero killed almost 6,000 bulls and was the founder of the Rondan School.

THE FAÇADE

Neo-classical with some Baroque detail. It consists of a semi pointed arch flanked by Tuscan columns supporting a split pediment with the shield of the Real Maestranza and a balcony with Rondan ironwork with images alluding to bull fights.

Its bullfighting museum is a permanent exhibition of two Rondan dynasties: Romeros and Ordóñez. There are also etchings, lithographs and drawings.... of the world of bullfighting and the history of the Real Maestranza. Of note: a Goyesque suit of lights of Antonio Ordóñez and a leather jerkin. In this photo taken in Ronda in 1959 we see Cayetano Ordóñez "Niño de la Palma", Ernest Hemingway and Antonio Ordóñez. To the left, Orson Welles, 1964. His ashes are in a well on the estate "El Recreo" belonging to the Ordóñez family.
Photo by Cuso.

• **GUADALEVÍN VALLEY,**

Seen from the gardens of the Alameda, beginning of the 19th century. They are the most important gardens in Ronda, where the Tajo reaches a depth of 177 mtrs. In these gardens there is the monument to the founder of the Rondan dynasty, Don Pedro Romero by the artist Vicente Bolós, 1954.

BLAS INFANTE PROMENADE AND ALAMEDA PARK

Tiled plaque to Blas Infante (1885 – 1936) Father of Historical Andalusism. In these gardens the Espinel Theatre was located (1909 – 1975) **Review of Historical Adalusism** At the side is the plaque commemorating the celebration of the first Georgista Hispano American Congress in 1913 on the unique tax and of the first Andalusian Assembly, 1918, marking the base of Historical Andalusism creating the Andalusian shield and the green and white flag.

At the entrance to the Alameda Gardens is the plaque to Orson Welles from the year 2000. His ashes were deposited on 7th May 1987 at his request, in the Recreo de San Cayetano, owned by the Ordóñez family, road to Campillos km. 1.

CHURCH - CONVENT OF LA MERCED. (photo right) This was founded and dedicated to Our Lady of Mercy by Los Mercedarios Order at the end of the 16th century. The church is Mannerist/Mudejar style. It has three naves although only the central one is used as the side naves have been sealed and have been converted into cells and rooms. The façade is constructed in masonry and exposed brick and on the side there is an octagonal tower with pilasters. Worthy of mention is the stone doorway with its half pointed arch. Above is a niche with the image of the founder of the order, St. Pedro Nolasco. From 1924 it has been occupied by the Carmelite Order.

•THE RELICS, *The left hand of St. Teresa of Jesus, the typical confectionary and the building's recent restoration in 1999 are justifiable reasons to visit this convent (photo below).*

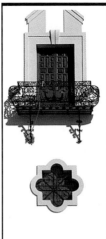

•**Church of the Socorro**
Before its destruction during the Civil War in 1936. Photo below

■ Church of the Socorro.

It was built on top of a primitive hermitage and was the royal residence of the Maestre (Master) of Calatrava during the conquest of the city. At the end of the 16th century a hospital for the poor and pilgrims was added to the original building. Hence its name Socorro. (Succour). At the beginning of the 18th century the original building was demolished and in its place a new church was built in 1709. In 1836 the parish was founded and later destroyed in 1936. The current church is a new building, completed in 1956. It is very representative of the construction policy at that time. On the tympanum of the façade, the imperial shield is embraced by the eagle of St. John.

• **Casino in Monterray style Artist's Circle,** late 19th century.

• **Plaza del Socorro**

It was created to give an open space for Rondans to walk during the long Winters and next to the Church of Socorro. The tree lined square has a fountain and at the end of the 19th century the large building of the Casino or Artist's Circle was built. The square has regained the space and beauty for which it was conceived, after its renovation in 1994. Modernism, introduced by the Rondan architect Santiago Sanguinetti (1875 – 1930) was to be the representative architecture for the Rondan middle class at the beginning of the 20th century. A perfect combination between the materials used and its decorative features. i.e. ironwork being the preferred material.

• **Plaza del Socorro,** *photo from 1944 (below)*

Below, relevant houses from Rondan modernism in the Plaza del Socorro.

• **Monument** to the illustrious Rondan Don Francisco Giner de los Rios (1839 – 1915), liberal intellectual and creator of the Institución Libre de Enseñanza. This square was the place for public executions during the 17th and 18th centuries.

• **Rondan Balcony,** (right) forged in 1793. Located in the Calle Espinel (Main Street).

• **Plaza de los Descalzos** Each year this small square holds the traditional fiestas on the night of St. John, or Fire Fiesta and the beginning of the Summer solstice.

• **The Church of los Descalzos,** parish of St. Cecilia, 1875, belonged to the monk's Order of the Trinitarios Descalzos (a Barefooted order) from 1663 to 1836. Its ground plan is a Latin cross with three naves, the central being the widest and is decorated with vegetal and human elements. It is separated from the other side naves by thick pillars with Corinthian pilasters supporting heavy, half pointed arches. The façade is a harmonious Baroque combination with a beautiful set of split pediments, one in the centre with side balconies and the doorway to the old convent. A raised atrium, enclosed by a thick Rondan ironwork grill completes its entrance.

• **CHAPEL OF THE VIRGEN DE LOS DOLORES (OUR LADY OF SORROWS)** *Below. Constructed during the reign of King Fernando VI in 1734. The chapel has a rectangular ground plan decorated in stone with sculptures of plants. On the front there is a niche with an image of the Virgen de los Dolores, but most original and striking are the Ionic columns where four embedded anthropomorphic figures are held to the column by rope around their neck. The interior figures look like bird men or fallen angels and those outside like humans, differentiated by their hair style and physical form. These figures fit the Mannerist spirit of the 18th century.*

• **LAS PEÑAS DISTRICT**

Going down the Calle Capitán Cortés, next to the Hospital Viejo de Santa Barbara, we find a beautiful network of streets which make up this district of Las Peñas. By taking any of the streets we arrive at the Calle Real, in the district of Padre Jesús and come across one of the lesser known sights of our walks through the city of Ronda. We discover a district of white houses, grills, geraniums, jasmins and emblazoned houses reminding us of the glory that was the main Calle Real during the 16th, 17th and 18th centuries. It is an introduction to that romantic of centuries, the 19th, a century of generous bandits, bull fighters, mule drivers, impoverished girls and smugglers from the mountains.

RONDA
in focus

A Visit of Ronda: Route 4
A walk through the San Francisco District.
San Sebastian Minaret.
The Church of The Espíritu Santo (Holy Ghost)
The Almocábar and Carlos V Gates
Rupestrian Church of Virgen de la Cabeza

Left, Rupestrian Church of Our Lady of La Cabeza

RIO GUADALEVÍN

zos

Cortés

C/ Virgen de los Dolores

Plaza
de la
Oscuriad

Calle

Rios

Calle

Claveros

Calle Real

Cuesta
de las
Piletas

C/ Méndez M.

Cantos

Monjas

Calle las

Santa

Cecilia

C/ Santa Cecilia

C/ Yeseros

Los

Vicentes

Plaza
Carmen
Abela

Calle

Calle

C/ Juan Pérez

Calle

de Guzmán

Remedios

Mina

la

Calle

Calle

sio

Calle

Rios

Rosas

Calle

las

Tiendas

Ánimas

los

Calle

Doña   Elvira

C/ Marques

de Salvatierra

Mural

S. Antonio

C/ Luz

Calle

C/ Aurora

Espinel

Calle

Nueva

Calle

Villanueva

Calle

Santo

Domingo

Calle

Ruedo

Pza.
de
Abul F

la

Paz

Plaza
de
España

C/ José Aparicio

Calle

Armiñán

0

J. de Cádiz

Plaza
El Gigante

C/ San Juan Bos

Tenorio

Holgado

C/ez. Campos

Plaza
Teniente
Arce

Blas   Infante

Plaza
Maria
Auxiliadora

Mirador
El Campillo

C/ José

C/ Sor Ángela de la Cruz

R. Gamero

M

TAJO DE RONDA

Muralla de la Albacara

RÍO   GUADALEVÍN

Puerta del Cristo

Puerta del Viento

4

Iglesia de la Virgen
de la Cabeza

ROUTE 4

- ⓪ A WALK THROUGH THE SAN FRANCISCO DISTRICT
- ① SAN SEBASTIAN MINARET
- ② HOLY GHOST CHURCH
- ③ ALMOCÁBAR AND CHARLES V GATES
- ④ RUPESTRIAN CHURCH OF VIRGEN DE LA CABEZA

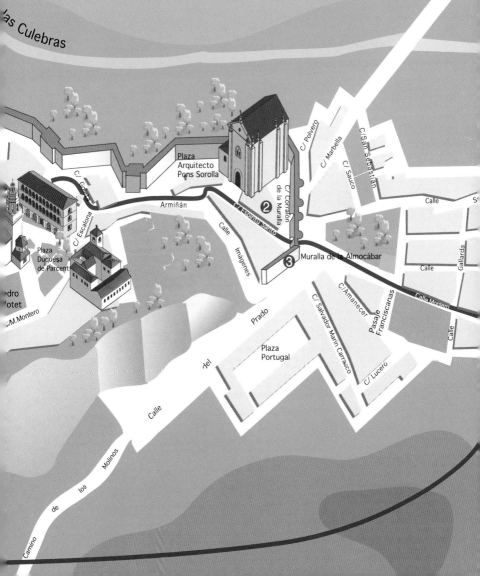

- **THE MINARET**

Is situated in the very attractive square of the Rondan poet, Abul Becca, 13th century.
It is the only preserved Arab Minaret in Ronda since the Reconquest. It is called the minaret because the mosque used to occupy this place until 1485. It became a parish church dedicated to St. Sebastian.

■ **THE SAN SEBASTIAN MINARET.**

Constructed in the 14th century under Nazarite domination, it consists of three bodies: the lower of stone ashlars with a horseshoe arch door and a lintel showing an interlaced design in stone and the remainder in green glazed ceramics. The central part is of exposed brick with two horseshoe arched small windows with interlaced brick geometrical decorations on each side. Finally the upper part from the Christian era, built as the church bell tower with four openings finished off with a double gabled Mudéjar roof of four slopes.

A WALK THROUGH THE DISTRICT OF SAN FRANCISCO

To discover a city one must understand it. It makes such an impression on us and a yearning to return.

• VIEW OF THE DISTRICT OF SAN FRANCISCO

Continuing along the street we find one of the most beautiful and best loved districts in Ronda, the district of San Francisco.

•THE CHURCH OF THE HOLY GHOST is the most representative monument. It was built by order of Fernando the Catholic King on top of the mosque which was in the Higher Suburb (Arrabal Alto), between 1485 and 1505. It is a Gothic buil-ding with Renaissance touches consisting of one single nave divided into two sections by a large triumphal arch. Its main Baroque altar practically covers all the central apse with a painting depicting, in its upper part, the arrival of the Holy Ghost and in the centre another on wood depicting in beautiful Byzantine style, the Virgen de la Antigua.

• THE CHURCH OF THE HOLY SPIRIT, to the left, an austere construction built during the reconquest of the Kingdom of Granada. It was completed in 1505, the year of the death of Queen Isabel the Catholic. It was Ronda's main church during the 16th and 17th centuries

• ALMOCÁBAR

This gateway takes its name from the Arabic word, "Al-maqâbir" or gateway to the cemetery. It was the main gate and gave access to the Alto District and Muslim Medina through the Imágenes Gate which is now non-existent.

In front of this is an esplanade which was used by the Arabs as a Musalla (a place for large religious events) and as a Musara (a place for exercising horses)

• **THE ALMOCÁBAR "AL-MAQÁBIR" GATE** or cemetery gate. Located in the southern part and the least protected area of the Madi-nat. It was built late 13th/early 14th century between two large semicircular masonry towers

with three arches, the two end ones being horseshoe shaped and the centre one Gothic style with an upper opening for the portcullis. During the middle of the 16th cen-tury during the time of King Carlos I, another crenalated, Renaissance gateway was added. It is a semi circular stone arch on which rests a royal shield supported by the Imperial eagle. In front of the gates is a large esplanade. Here we find the small church of Nuestra Sra. de Gracia (Our Lady of Grace) patron saint of the Real Maestranza de Caballería de Ronda. (Equestrian Society of Spanish Noblemen).

Taking the road towards Algeciras, when you reach Pila de Doña Gaspara turn right and follow the peaceful and pleasant road for approx. 30 minutes. It will lead you to the Virgen de la Cabeza, enjoying all the time incomparable views of the city, built on a defiant giant rock, inspiring in their time sensitive souls such as Reiner Maria Rilke or David Bomberg.

• **PILGRIMAGE**
On the second Sunday in June. An 18th century image has been paraded for a long time with great popular devotion as patron saint of Ronda. It is a time when many Rondans get together and carry the statue of their Virgen away to the countryside of Ronda.
Photo left.

CHURCH OF NUESTRA SEÑORA DE LA CABEZA

It was built in the same sandstone excavated by the hermits or monastic communities between the 9th and 10th centuries and used by Mozarab communities in Ronda during Muslim domination. The church is of basilican style with two sections. One dedicated to worship and the other to monastic living. The main part, dedicated to worship, consists of a central nave where there is a main altar and three naves perpendicular to it. The sacristy has stone niches to hold images and under the altar is a crypt.

ROUTE 5

FIRST DAY:
EXCURSION THROUGH THE SIERRA DE LAS NIEVES-NATURAL PARK.

SECOND DAY:
EXCURSION THROUGH THE UPPER GENAL VALLEY
CARTAJIMA
IGUALEJA
PUJERRA
JÚZCAR
FARAJÁN
ALPANDEIRE
ATAJATE

THIRD DAY:
EXCURSION THROUGH THE WHITE VILLAGES
ARRIATE
SETENIL
ACINIPO "RONDA LA VIEJA"
TORRE ALHÁQUIME
OLVERA-SANCTUARY OF OUR LADY OF THE REMEDIOS
ZAHARA DE LA SIERRA
GRAZALEMA AND ITS NATURAL PARK
MONTEJAQUE
BENAOJÁN
CUEVA DE LA PILETA (PILETA CAVE)

Photo left Cartajima sliding down its cliffs

EXCURSION THROUGH THE SIERRA DE LAS NIEVES NATURAL PARK

•THE SILENCE *The silence all around us is broken by the majestic flight of the royal eagle or by the furtive flight of the peregrine falcon which are so abundant in the area.*
Numerous herds of mountain goats, with one or two deer, delight us on the pathways in the park. Also, the very likely and fortunate encounter with foxes and mongoose complete this day in the mountains.

• SPANISH FIR, *Abies Boissier (photo right)*

Excursion through the Sierra de las Nieves Natural Park. Leaving the district of San Francisco, towards the Costa del Sol, A376, we take the San Pedro de Alcántara road to gradually come across the impressive limestone masses of the Sierra Hidalga, Melequetín and Oreganal and in the background the Torrecilla de Sierra de las Nieves which at 1.919 mts. is the highest point in the area and in the province of Málaga.
All this mountainous, leafy woods and rich vegetation is the Sierra de las Nieves Natural Park. Visiting this park is very gratifying and will take at least a day's excursion. To get there continue along the road towards

Marbella until arriving at km. 13: turn to the left (road in good condition) and follow the sign for Rajete or Sierra de las Nieves Natural Park. Two and a half kms. later the road divides into two; take the left turn. Continue, leaving on the right the country house of La Nava de San Luis; we immediately find the gate that stops the

mountain goats escaping from the park; open it and then carefully close it again, then take the path which leads to los Queji-gales Refuge. From there you can easily walk through the park. Any path we take will lead us to disco-ver unfor-gettable landscapes. Either the Peñón de

Ronda path (1.286 mts.), on the left, or the main route on the right will take us to the summit of la Torre-cilla (1.919 mts.) This second path is interesting and instructive. We will find the largest expanse of Spanish firs (Pinsapos Abies Bois-

accompanied by splendid woods of walnut, pines and ash trees and interesting specimens of the conifer family, such as yew. We are always surrounded by aromatic plants, abundant in this mountain range, such as the rock rose, thyme and rosemary. Rea-ching the summit of the Torrecilla we will enjoy an impressive view of the Costa del Sol from Gibraltar to Fuengirola, and on its north eastern face we will discover the chapel of Nuestra Señora de las Nie-ves, 16th century and at the bottom of its steep slopes the towns of El Burgo and Yunquera. On clear days our eyes can even make out the Atlas Range in North Africa or the white peaks of the Sierra Nevada.

Very possible encounters with foxes or mongoose.... will complete an unforget-table day in this paradise of our mountain range.

• **THE SIERRA DE LAS NIEVES,** *declared a biosphere reserve by UNESCO, currently has the largest expanse of Spanish firs in Mediterranean Europe, a tertiary age species, or pri-mitive fir, endemic to the Iberian peninsula.*

sier) i n Medite-rranean Europe. During the ascent we will be

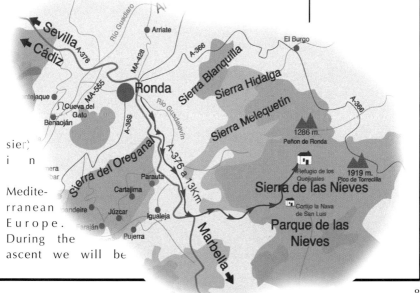

•THE GENAL VALLEY *is an explosion of colours and contrasts of culture and traditions. The farming of chestnuts and vegetables, bars and restaurants with good food, as well as rural accommodation are the main income for this paradisiacal valley.*
Its musts, spirits, breadcrumbs fried in garlic and pork products are recommended.

EXCURSION THROUGH THE UPPER GENAL VALLEY

Retake the Costa del Sol road; 10 kms. from Ronda on the right we find the sign for the

Igualeja – Pujerra. Take the Igualeja direction across some arid limestone hills; when the road narrows we come across a panorama of vivid reds, yellows and greens with a small white villa-

ge which looks as if it is rolling down the mountain side. This is Cartajima and it is worthy of mention as it was thus named by King Fernando VII.

The next town to appear before our eyes is Igualeja. It is well know for its hardworking and fun loving people and because at the entrance to the village, on the left, is the source of the Genal river which forms the valley which we will get to know as one of the few preserved natural paradises of Andalusia.

Follow the road which takes us to Pujerra. For 6 kms. we are constantly invited to stop and admire the 100 year old chestnut trees. Pujerra has 320 inhabitants and like many other villages in the area it concentrates on timber industry and pig and goat farming. We retake the road which returns to Igualeja and in one km. on the left we take the forest road to Júzcar. The silent descent to

• **THE VILLAGE OF CARTAJIMA** *(photo above) Surrounded by chestnut , holm oaks and cork oak woods; its population of about 325 devotes itself to wood production and the farming of chestnuts. It is a good spot for weekend breaks and hiking. It has good rural accommodation and picturesque bars so that we can try some of the cuisine and mountain products.*

• IGUALEJA

As with the majority of the towns in the area its origin is Berber. It has a prosperous population of appox. 1,100 inhabitants who are mainly dedicated to the production and marketing of chestnuts, pork products and other crafts. Its traditional representation of the Passion of Holy week, its fiestas for San Gregorio at the end of August and the Toro de Fuego (Bull of Fire) fiesta are famous.

the Genal river is accompanied by cork oaks, holm oaks and chestnuts. On arrival at the river you will find a clear water course which is today a fishing reserve with remains of old mills, market gardens, orange and other fruit trees and the sensation that we are in a paradisiacal spot.

We continue towards Júzcar, breaking the descent to look at the village of Pujerra, 770mts. and in the background the village of Jubrique. The village of Jubrique with 900 inhabitants, in the distance looks more like a white stain of chalk amongst cotton trees. In its time of

splendour it had wine cellars, spirit distilleries and mining. Today like the other villages in the area it is involved in the industrialization and export of chestnuts. Its historical importance in the Genal valley is due to its church of San Francisco, an old Arab mosque.

We arrive at Júzcar. It is a small village like Pujerra with approx. 250 inhabitants, also dedicated to the chestnut with some cultivations, such as vines, vegetables and olives. Next to the river was the Royal Tin Plate Factory during the reign of King Felipe V, at the beginning of the 18th century.

Wine and spirit production was the main income for the majority of these villages in the past. We can enjoy an exquisite must in any of them during the months of November and December. We continue towards the left until we arrive at the "delightful" village of Fara-ján, as its Arab name states. The landscape appears to change from leafy chestnut woods to a mountainous area of thicket and rockrose, where pork and goat far-ming are common. Its current population of 315 is involved in the harves-ting of chestnuts and animal farming. It is an excellent place to try the cured

ham and the good home-made cuisine. One eats well in Casa Remedios. The villa-ge must have been very rich and important in this area as the numerous preserved religious buildings show us. E.g. The church of Our Lady of the Rosary from early 16th century, Church of San Sebastian, Hermitage of the Santo Niño (Holy Infant) and the Carmelite Convent.

We continue now, taking the road towards Alpandeire. We see that the landscape changes; we pass from the green and red chestnut woods to the white and greys of the limestone, from wood-land fertility to dry uncul-tivated land. Alpandeire is a town

• **PUJERRA,** *(above) It is a white pearl among a leafy colourful chestnut wood.*

• **ONE HUNDRED YEAR OLD CHEST-NUT TREE,** *left. On the road that joins Igualeja with Puje-rra.*

• **ALPANDEIRE**,
photo above. To stop in the square is to contemplate in the distance the chain of white villages that make up the Genal Valley.

because the title was granted by King Fernando VII and it has a large church for the parish of St. Anthony. It is a parish church from the 16th century and restored in the 18th century. It stands out like a great cathedral within the humble urbanism

of its surroundings. The town has a population of approx. 320 inhabitants living off pig and goat farming and some poor agriculture. It is also the birthplace of the miraculous monk, Friar Leopoldo de Alpandeire and many of his faithful make

pilgrimages to the area. Its confectionary made with oil, rabbit in tomato sauce, and wild asparagus omelettes are exquisite.

We leave this town, one of the first to be founded by the Arabs in our mountain range and immediately we see in the bare and dry landscape the sign on the left for Villafría, the house where Friar Leopoldo of Alpandeire lived. There is a brusque change. Sinuous curves across a bare environment bring us to the edge of the Sierra de los Perdigones. We arrive at the crossroads with the Ronda – Algeciras road A369. If we take the right turn we will again be in the city of Ronda in ten minutes time. If we take the left we will get to know the valley of the Lower Genal with villages such as Atajate, Benadalid, Benalauría, Algatocín, Benarrabá, or Gaucín.

•**Atajate,** *150 inhabitants.*
It had a castle and was an important village on the Algeciras – Gibraltar road towards Ronda. It was a path for smugglers, timewasters, backpackers, mule leaders, thugs and tyrants together with romantic poets and adventurers. Its Must Festival at the end of November is an invitation to visit this tranquil spot.

•**Júzcar,** *photo below*

•THE ROUTE

The route is easy and relaxing, through countryside of olive trees scattered with white country houses and farm houses, with herds of Iberian pigs, goats and sheep amongst holm oaks and cork oaks. It is a route which shows the life of our farming villages characterised by their cordiality and simplicity.

We leave Ronda by the Campillos road, A- 367, and immediately turn left, MA428 towards Arriate. Its origin comes from the Arabic, "Arriadh" which means hamlet. It has been a town since 1661 and currently has a population of 3,450 inhabitants. Its elaboration of excellent pork products,

the manufacture of artisan furniture and the production of olive oil make it a productive and hardworking town. Worthy of mention is its tradition of hand bell ringing, especially at dawn, during Holy Week or the fiesta of its patron, St. Peter, plus its famous fiesta called "Partir la Vieja" on the first day of Lent. We leave Arriate to continue

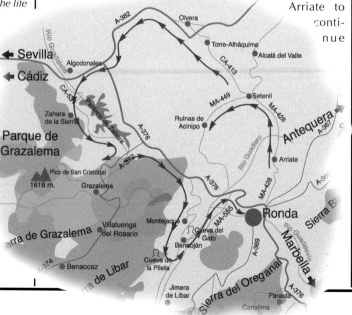

through the Rondan municipal districts of la Cimada and los Prados to arrive at the boundary of the province of Malaga. We enter into the province of Cadiz to arrive at Setenil. In front of us, in the distance, 18 kms. away, is Olvera surrounded by hills of holm oaks and olives. We arrive at the Guadalporcún river, turn left and discover an isolated town, Setenil de las Bodegas.

The Catholic Monarchs considered this a Royal town. It has 3,115 inhabitants.

It is an amazing town where whole streets have been made under over hanging rock marked by humidity and history. Its caves, old, fresh and deep cellars have been turned into white houses set into the stone. In the top part of Setenil, to the right, the CA413 road will take us to Olvera and to the left

OLVERA
Photo above. Old seat of the Dukes of Osuna, it became a key point during the reconquest as a border town between upper and lower Andalusia, as shown by its fortress/castle. It is a pilgrimage destination for many Andalusians, not so much for its splendid neo-classical parish church, finished in the middle of the 19th century, but for the shrine of the miraculous patron saint, Virgen de los Remedios, situated outside the walls, and from the 16th century.

To the left, Setenil de las Bodegas

• **SETENIL DE LAS BODEGAS,**
*photo above.
Situated on the edge of the province of Cadiz and surrounded by Malaga province. The town is in an elevated position defended by its solid walls whose history has developed with that of Ronda and its region. It was conquered by the Catholic Monarchs in September 1484.*

To the right, the Roman theatre of Acinipo surrounded by piles of rocks and taegulae. Its seats are carved into the rock.

the road leads to Acinipo and the town of Gastor, the balcony of Andalusia. Let us visit Acinipo. In just 2 kms. to the left, we find the MA449 road taking us to the ruins of Acinipo, Land of Wine or Ronda la Vieja (Old Ronda) It is situated at 800 mts. above sea level, in the heart of Roman Andalusia. It became a municipality with the power to mint its own coins and its inhabitants had the same rights as any citizen of Imperial Rome. At its entrance, on the right, there are Iberian remains belonging to a Bronze Age people from the 8th and 7th century BC.

We return to the town of Setenil and take the Setenil – Torre Alháquime – Olvera road, CA413. It is a narrow, well surfaced road accompanied all the way by the River Guadalporcún until it reaches at the village of Torre Alháquime. This village of 924 inhabitants, on the Banditry route, is like a painting of white houses advertising our Andalusia. Land of Bandits and mountain people, watchtower and frontier between the kingdoms of Seville and Granada until its conquest by King Alfonso XI. A great mosaic at its entrance with the legend of José Maria Hinojosa

"El Tempranillo" makes us stop. "The King rules in Spain and I rule in the mountains" Its parish church of la Virgen de la Antigua, 18th century, its remains of the Arab fortress and a stroll through its white and tranquil streets are obligatory reasons to stop for a while.

After just 5 kms. we shall arrive at Olvera, 8,715 inhabitants. After a short visit to its fortress and churches we take the A382 road towards Jerez de la Frontera. After 14 kms. of good road we leave, on the right, the village of Algodonales and we immediately take the left, regional road CA351, which takes us across the reservoir

towards the town of Zahara de la Sierra.

It has a population of 1.580 inhabitants and was an obligatory pass for people, animals and goods on the border between the kingdoms of Seville and Granada. Still preserved are the old clocktower from the 16th century and its 13th century castle.

We leave Zahara and take the road marked Arroyo Molino. This road takes us right along the edge of the reservoir, made in 1991, between herds of goats and sheep whose cheese is known around the world. We follow the old Seville-Ronda road and stop at the

•**ZAHARA DE LA SIE-RRA,** *photo above.*

Its steep streets decorated with orange and lemon trees; the houses clinging to the hillside; the castle with its diverse history; magnificent views of the reservoir and its mild climate due to the protection from the Grazalema mountains of the natural park, all make a leisurely visit worthwhile.

• GRAZALEMA, *This is the area with the highest rainfall in Spain with an average of 2,000mm/year.*

N° S DE LOS REMEDIOS

• OLVERA, *Our Lady of the Remedios, photo above.*
• ALCORNOQUE, *(cork tree), to the right. On the road that joins Ronda with Grazalema.*

very traditional and typical Venta el Tropezón to taste its cheese, pork loin or sausage in lard.

In our climb to the mountain pass of Montejaque, 705 mts. the Grazalema Natural Park accompanies us as far as the crossroad of the A372 road. Grazalema 2,490 inhabitants. Its fiestas of the Toro de Cuerda (The Rope Bull), its church of the Virgen de la Estrella (Our Lady of the Stars) 18th century, its peaceful streets and enchanting corners with a steep landscape, full of holm oaks, cork oaks, gall oaks and carob trees accompanied by scrub land plants like the rock rose or gorse and

medicinal plants like oregano or lavender, populated by deer, fox and genets; as well as having one of the biggest colonies of tawny vultures in Spain obliges us to plan a trip exclusively to this town and its park. We immediately come across

the A376 road. We turn right after 300 mts. and take the MA505 towards Montejaque – Benaoján. Through a beautiful gall oak wood leaving on the right the empty reservoir of Montejaque and the entrance to the Hundidero Cave, which forms part of and links with the Cueva del Gato (The Cave of the Cat), we then arrive at Montejaque.

A town of Arab origin and old seat of the Counts of Bena-vente, it currently has a population of 950 inhabitants. We make our way up Mure Hill until we reach the village of Benaoján. It currently has a population of 1,615 inhabitants and was also the old seat of the Counts of Benavente. The pork product industry is the main income for the population. At the entrance to the town we take the road to the right which leads to Pileta Cave -Cortes de la Fron-

•**MONTEJAQUE,**
The town is set into the Sierra del Hacho which means "Lost mountain". It is a string of white houses hanging over the mountain sides.

• CUEVA DE LA PILETA, *Declared a national monument in 1924. Visits to the cave are very restricted and last approximately one hour. Its majestic limestone caves and galleries created by nature, together with the stalactites, form chambers for the bats, the Cathedral, the Dead Woman, the Fish, the Organ... Some of them, in red and yellow are between 12,000 and 15,000 years old. However, above all, its fame is due to the extraordinary paintings and engravings in the Shrine chamber and the Fish chamber. The Shrine chamber is the most outstanding place in the caves because of the perfection of its paintings; the two human figures and the fourteen Paleolithic representations of the Solutrense, the pregnant mare being the most representative.*

tera, MA505, and, through cuttings and crags, after 4 kms. we arrive at the mausoleum of Andalusian Prehistory, the Pileta Cave. We return to the village of Benaoján, turn to the right and take the MA555 road, which takes us towards Ronda. We cross the River Guadiaro leaving on our left the Algeciras – Bobadilla railway. What a beautiful train journey from Ronda to Algeciras! Two hours there and two hours back across a unique region: la Almoraima, las Saucedas, los Alcornocales park... an unforgettable journey with its 19th century Victorian stations and

memories of smugglers and romantic English people. We continue along the river, leaving on the left The Cueva del Gato. We could stop at any of the little bars along this road to recover strength. Country houses and fields of vegetables until we arrive at the military installations of the IV Regiment of the Legion.

Finally we come across the Seville – Ronda road A376. We turn right and 2 kms. away is the town of Ronda.